Christmas Piano Ensembles

Four-part student ensembles with conductor's score and optional accompaniments

Arranged by Phillip Keveren

TABLE OF CONTENTS

Christmas Piano Ensembles Level 4 is designed for use with the fourth book of most piano methods.

Concepts in *Christmas Piano Ensembles Level 4*:

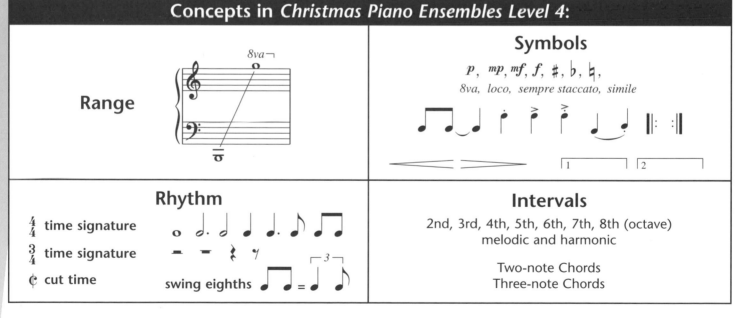

Range

Symbols

p, mp, mf, f, ♯, ♭, ♮,
8va, *loco*, *sempre staccato*, *simile*

Rhythm

$\frac{4}{4}$ time signature
$\frac{3}{4}$ time signature
¢ cut time
swing eighths

Intervals

2nd, 3rd, 4th, 5th, 6th, 7th, 8th (octave)
melodic and harmonic

Two-note Chords
Three-note Chords

Editor: J. Mark Baker

ISBN 0-634-05121-0

HAL•LEONARD® CORPORATION

7777 W. BLUEMOUND RD. P.O. BOX 13819 MILWAUKEE, WI 53213

Copyright © 2004 by HAL LEONARD CORPORATION
International Copyright Secured   All Rights Reserved

For all works contained herein:
Unauthorized copying, arranging, adapting, recording or public performance is an infringement of copyright.
Infringers are liable under the law.

Visit Hal Leonard Online at
www.halleonard.com

Foreword

Piano study doesn't need to be lonely any more! These ensemble versions of favorite Christmas songs will give students the pleasure and inspiration of playing with their friends.

Each selection includes:
- A conductor's score with optional teacher accompaniment

- Four student parts:
  Parts I and II for the first piano
  Parts III and IV for the second piano

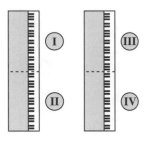

Four players at two pianos will be able to give a full and appropriate performance of each piece, yet more combinations of players and instruments are possible. Students can even add an orchestra!

Here are some ideas:
- Use four digital pianos or electronic keyboards that allow students to play the suggested instrumentation for each part.

- Double, triple, or quadruple the student parts.*

- Add the orchestral arrangement available on CD 💿 or GM disk 💾 .

- Add the optional teacher accompaniment, designed for both rehearsal and performance, by using an additional piano or keyboard.

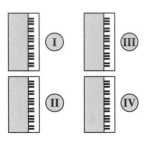

Full orchestral arrangements, available on CD #00296346 or GM disk #00296351, may be used for both performance and rehearsal:

 The **first** and **second** track numbers are two different **practice** tempos, the second one slightly faster than the first. The **third** track number is the **performance** tempo.

 The GM disk has only **one track per title** and is a preset **performance** tempo. GM disk tracks can be slowed down to any **practice** tempo desired, and can also be made faster than the "set" performance tempo at will.

If students are using a digital keyboard that lacks a suggested sound, other voices may be substituted. For example, if an instrument does not have "Glockenspiel," use any available similar sound, such as "Vibes" or "Marimba." If "Oboe" is unavailable, use any similar sustaining sound, such as "Flute," "Clarinet," or "Strings."

I hope you and your students will enjoy the challenges and pleasures of playing these exciting ensembles. Strike up the piano band!

Phillip Keveren

Due to copyright restrictions, it will be necessary to buy a new book for every four parts.

Angels We Have Heard On High

Conductor's Score & Optional Accompaniment

Performance Configurations

Two Pianos

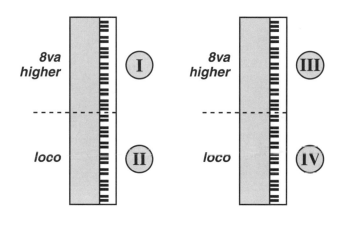

OR

Four Keyboards
(with suggested instrumentation)

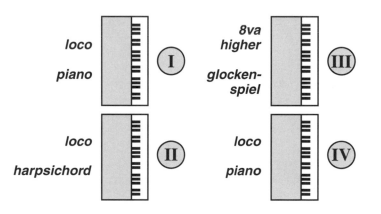

Angels We Have Heard On High

Traditional French Carol
Arranged by Phillip Keveren

Copyright © 2004 by HAL LEONARD CORPORATION
International Copyright Secured   All Rights Reserved

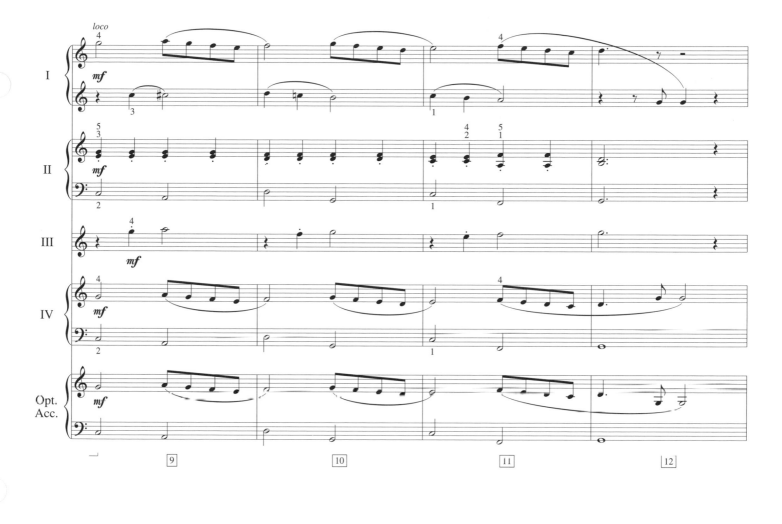

(1'28")

Jingle-Bell Rock
Conductor's Score & Optional Accompaniment

Performance Configurations

Two Pianos

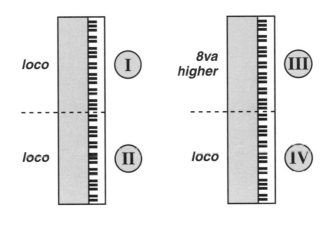

OR

Four Keyboards
(with suggested instrumentation)

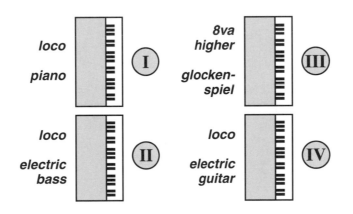

Jingle-Bell Rock

Music by Joe Beal
and Jim Boothe
Arranged by Phillip Keveren

Copyright © 1957 by Chappell & Co.
Copyright Renewed
This arrangement Copyright © 2004 by Chappell & Co.
International Copyright Secured   All Rights Reserved

9 Christmas Piano Ensembles – Level 4

Christmas Piano Ensembles – Level 4

If you are:
- sharing the keyboard with *Part II*, **play one octave higher**.
- seated at your own keyboard, **play as written**.

Suggested instrumentation:
piano

Angels We Have Heard On High

Part I

Traditional French Carol
Arranged by Phillip Keveren

Copyright © 2004 by HAL LEONARD CORPORATION
International Copyright Secured   All Rights Reserved

DO NOT PHOTOCOPY

Christmas Piano Ensembles – Level 4

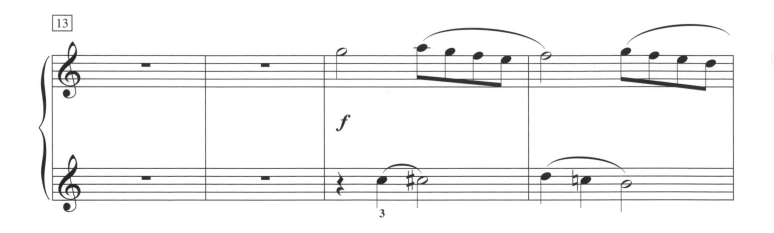

 DO NOT PHOTOCOPY

If you are:
- sharing the keyboard with *Part II*, **play as written**.
- seated at your own keyboard, **play as written**.

Suggested instrumentation: **piano**

Jingle-Bell Rock
Part I

Music by Joe Beal
and Jim Boothe
Arranged by Phillip Keveren

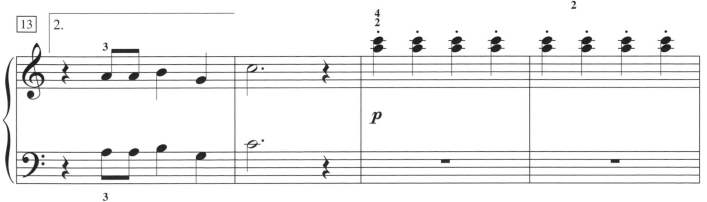

Copyright © 1957 by Chappell & Co.
Copyright Renewed
This arrangement Copyright © 2004 by Chappell & Co.
International Copyright Secured   All Rights Reserved

DO NOT PHOTOCOPY

Christmas Piano Ensembles – Level 4

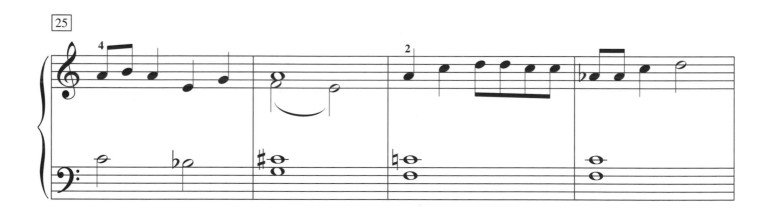

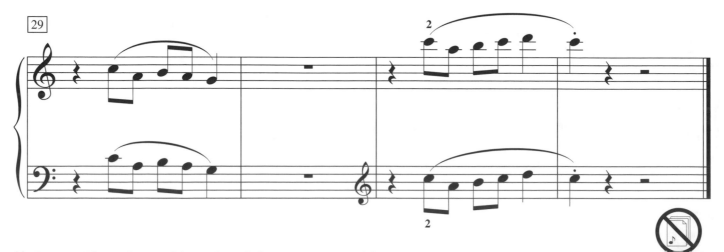

DO NOT PHOTOCOPY

If you are:
• sharing the keyboard with *Part I*, **play as written**.
• seated at your own keyboard, **play as written**.

Suggested instrumentation:
harpsichord

Angels We Have Heard On High

Part II

Traditional French Carol
Arranged by Phillip Keveren

Allegretto (♩ = 120)

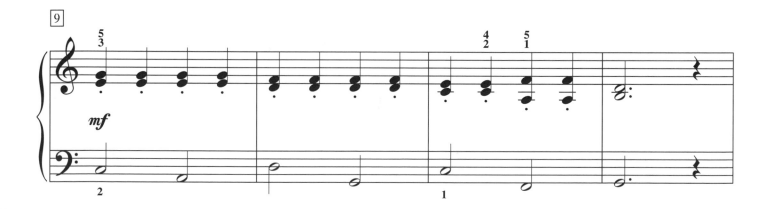

DO NOT PHOTOCOPY

Copyright © 2004 by HAL LEONARD CORPORATION
International Copyright Secured   All Rights Reserved

Christmas Piano Ensembles – Level 4

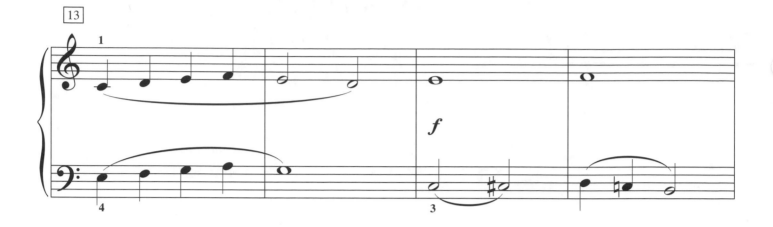

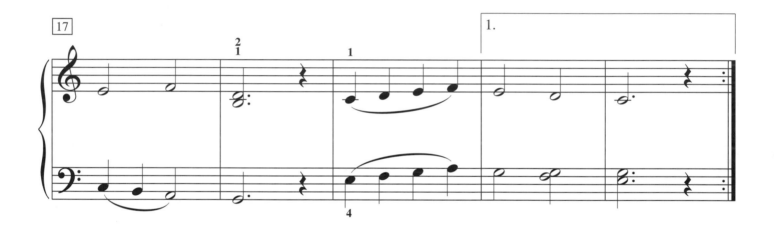

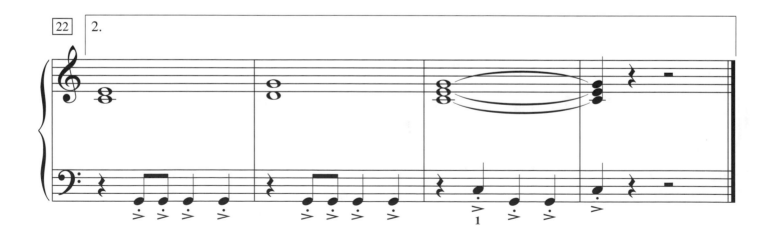

DO NOT PHOTOCOPY

Copyright © 1957 by Chappell & Co.
Copyright Renewed
This arrangement Copyright © 2004 by Chappell & Co.
International Copyright Secured   All Rights Reserved

DO NOT PHOTOCOPY

If you are:
- sharing the keyboard with *Part IV*, **play one octave higher**.
- seated at your own keyboard, **play one octave higher**.

Suggested instrumentation: **glockenspiel**

Angels We Have Heard On High

Part III

Traditional French Carol
Arranged by Phillip Keveren

Copyright © 2004 by HAL LEONARD CORPORATION
International Copyright Secured   All Rights Reserved

DO NOT PHOTOCOPY

Jingle-Bell Rock
Part III

If you are:
- sharing the keyboard with *Part IV*, **play one octave higher**.
- seated at your own keyboard, **play one octave higher**.

Suggested instrumentation: **glockenspiel**

Music by Joe Beal
and Jim Boothe
Arranged by Phillip Keveren

Brightly (♩ = 72)

Copyright © 1957 by Chappell & Co.
Copyright Renewed
This arrangement Copyright © 2004 by Chappell & Co.
International Copyright Secured All Rights Reserved

DO NOT PHOTOCOPY

If you are:
- sharing the keyboard with *Part III*, **play as written.**
- seated at your own keyboard, **play as written.**

Suggested instrumentation:
piano

Angels We Have Heard On High

Part IV

Traditional French Carol
Arranged by Phillip Keveren

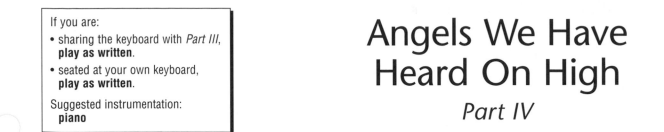

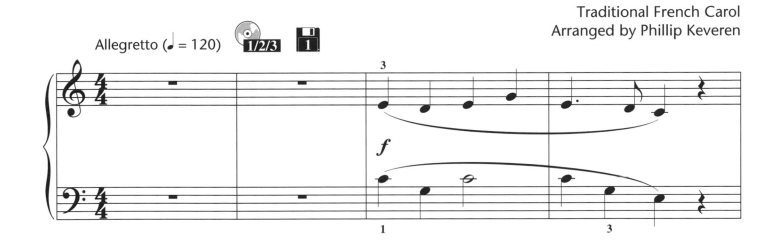

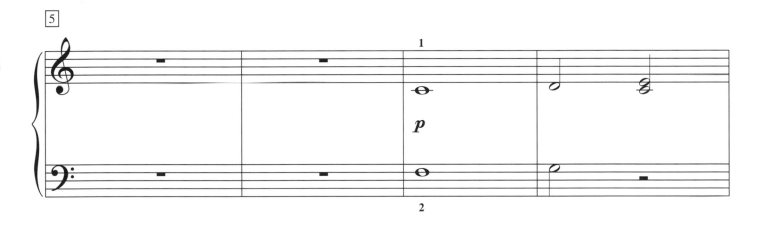

DO NOT PHOTOCOPY

Copyright © 2004 by HAL LEONARD CORPORATION
International Copyright Secured   All Rights Reserved

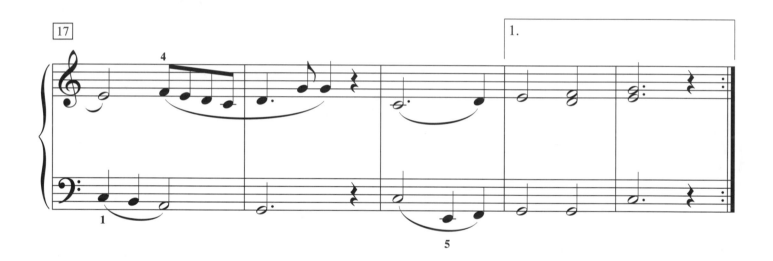

DO NOT PHOTOCOPY

If you are:
• sharing the keyboard with *Part III*, **play as written.**
• seated at your own keyboard, **play as written.**

Suggested instrumentation: **electric guitar**

Jingle-Bell Rock
Part IV

Music by Joe Beal
and Jim Boothe
Arranged by Phillip Keveren

Copyright © 1957 by Chappell & Co.
Copyright Renewed
This arrangement Copyright © 2004 by Chappell & Co.
International Copyright Secured   All Rights Reserved

DO NOT PHOTOCOPY

Christmas Piano Ensembles – Level 4

Parade Of The Wooden Soldiers

Conductor's Score & Optional Accompaniment

Performance Configurations

Two Pianos

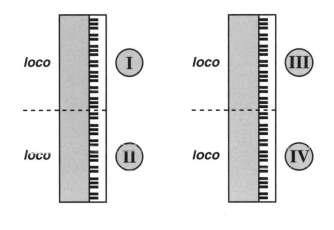

OR

Four Keyboards
(with suggested instrumentation)

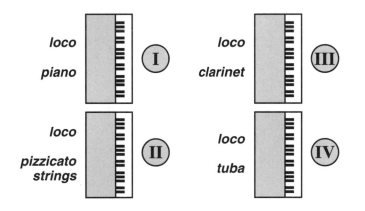

Parade Of The Wooden Soldiers

Music by Leon Jessel
Arranged by Phillip Keveren

Copyright © 2004 by HAL LEONARD CORPORATION
International Copyright Secured   All Rights Reserved

29   Christmas Piano Ensembles – Level 4

Christmas Piano Ensembles – Level 4

(1'19")

33   Christmas Piano Ensembles – Level 4

Silver Bells
Conductor's Score & Optional Accompaniment

Performance Configurations

Two Pianos

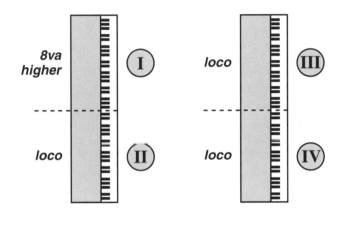

OR

Four Keyboards
(with suggested instrumentation)

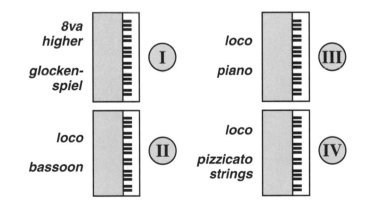

Silver Bells
from the Paramount Picture THE LEMON DROP KID

Music by Jay Livingston
and Ray Evans
Arranged by Phillip Keveren

Copyright © 1950 (Renewed 1977) by Paramount Music Corporation
This arrangement Copyright © 2004 by Paramount Music Corporation
International Copyright Secured   All Rights Reserved

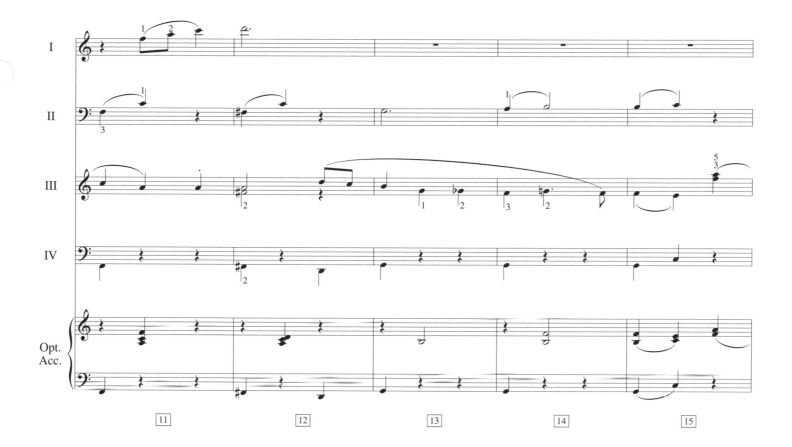

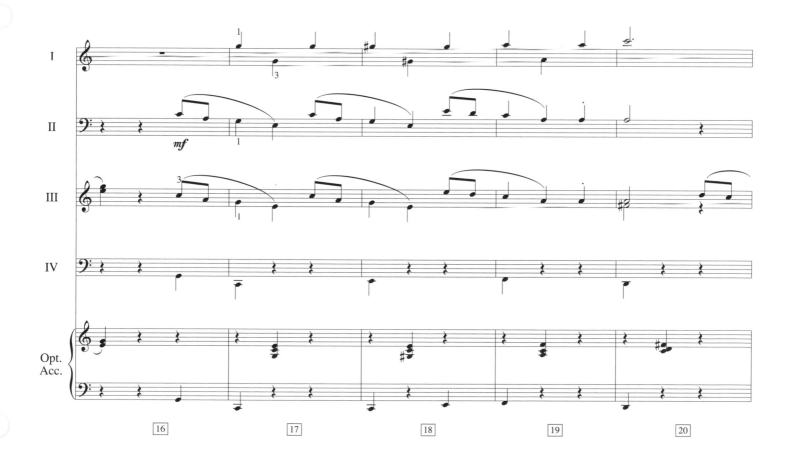

37   Christmas Piano Ensembles – Level 4

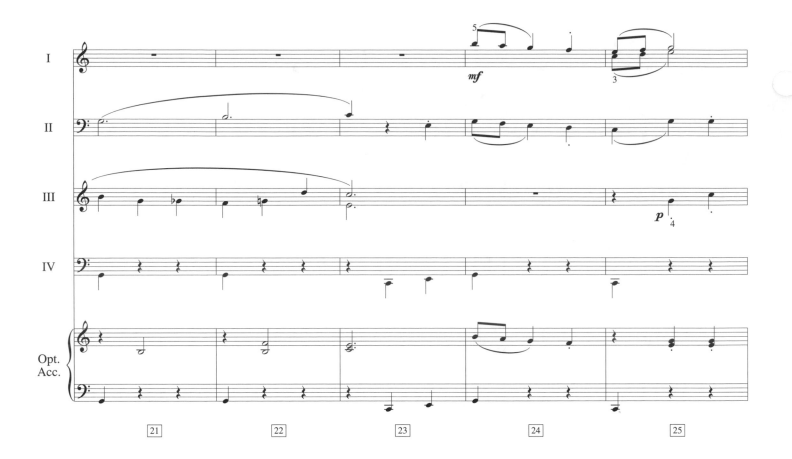

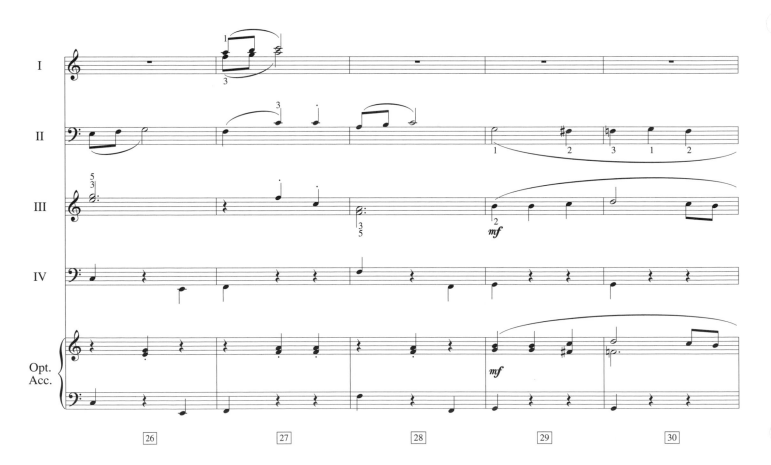

(57")

Christmas Piano Ensembles – Level 4

If you are:
- sharing the keyboard with *Part II*, **play as written**.
- seated at your own keyboard, **play as written**.

Suggested instrumentation:
piano

Parade Of The Wooden Soldiers

Part I

Music by Leon Jessel
Arranged by Phillip Keveren

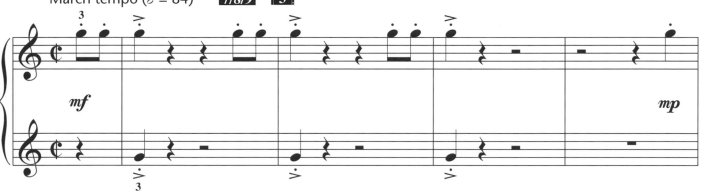

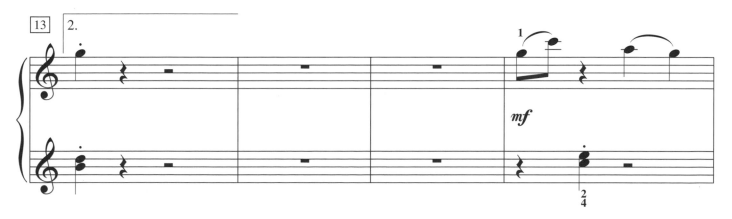

Copyright © 2004 by HAL LEONARD CORPORATION
International Copyright Secured   All Rights Reserved

DO NOT PHOTOCOPY

Christmas Piano Ensembles – Level 4

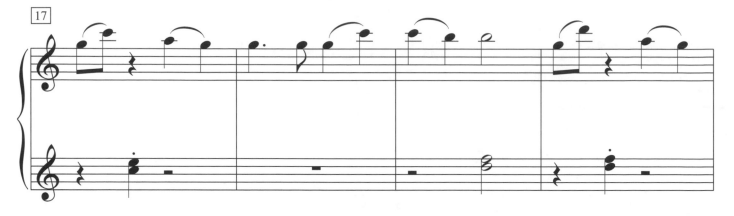

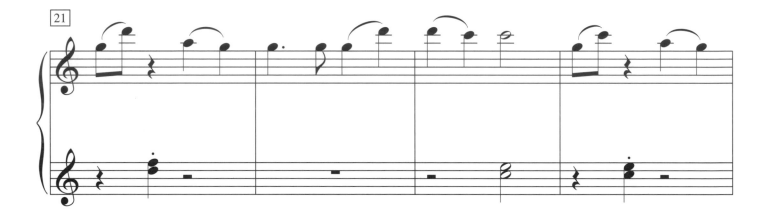

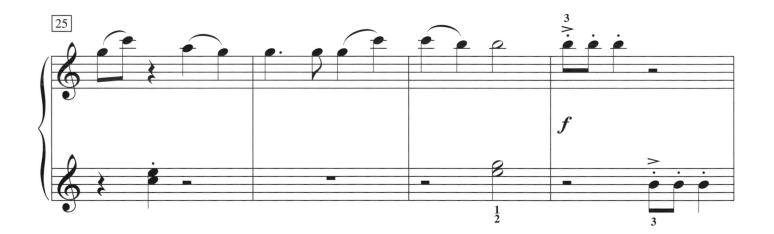

DO NOT PHOTOCOPY

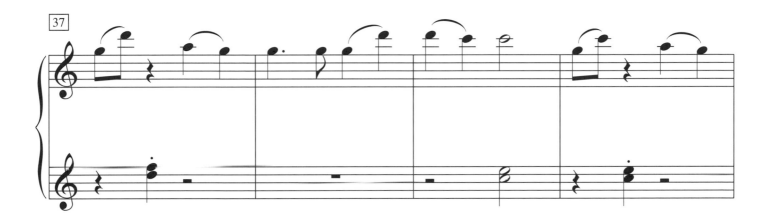

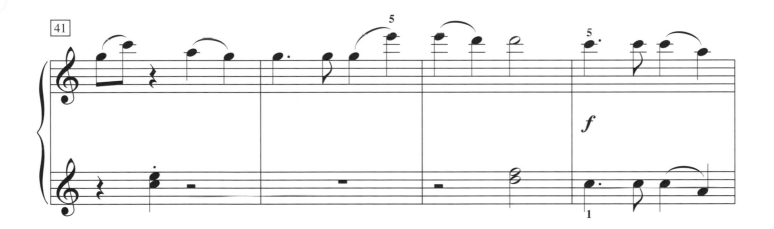

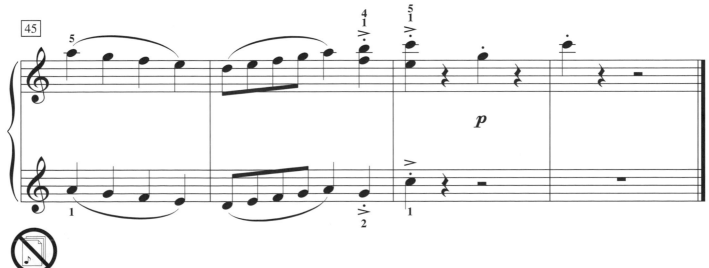

DO NOT PHOTOCOPY

Christmas Piano Ensembles – Level 4

Silver Bells
from the Paramount Picture THE LEMON DROP KID

Part I

If you are:
- sharing the keyboard with *Part II*, **play one octave higher**.
- seated at your own keyboard, **play one octave higher**.

Suggested instrumentation: **glockenspiel**

Music by Jay Livingston
and Ray Evans
Arranged by Phillip Keveren

Copyright © 1950 (Renewed 1977) by Paramount Music Corporation
This arrangement Copyright © 2004 by Paramount Music Corporation
International Copyright Secured   All Rights Reserved

DO NOT PHOTOCOPY

If you are:
- sharing the keyboard with *Part I*, **play as written**.
- seated at your own keyboard, **play as written**.

Suggested instrumentation: **pizzicato strings**

Parade Of The Wooden Soldiers

Part II

Music by Leon Jessel
Arranged by Phillip Keveren

March tempo (♩ = 84)

sempre staccato

Copyright © 2004 by HAL LEONARD CORPORATION
International Copyright Secured   All Rights Reserved

DO NOT PHOTOCOPY

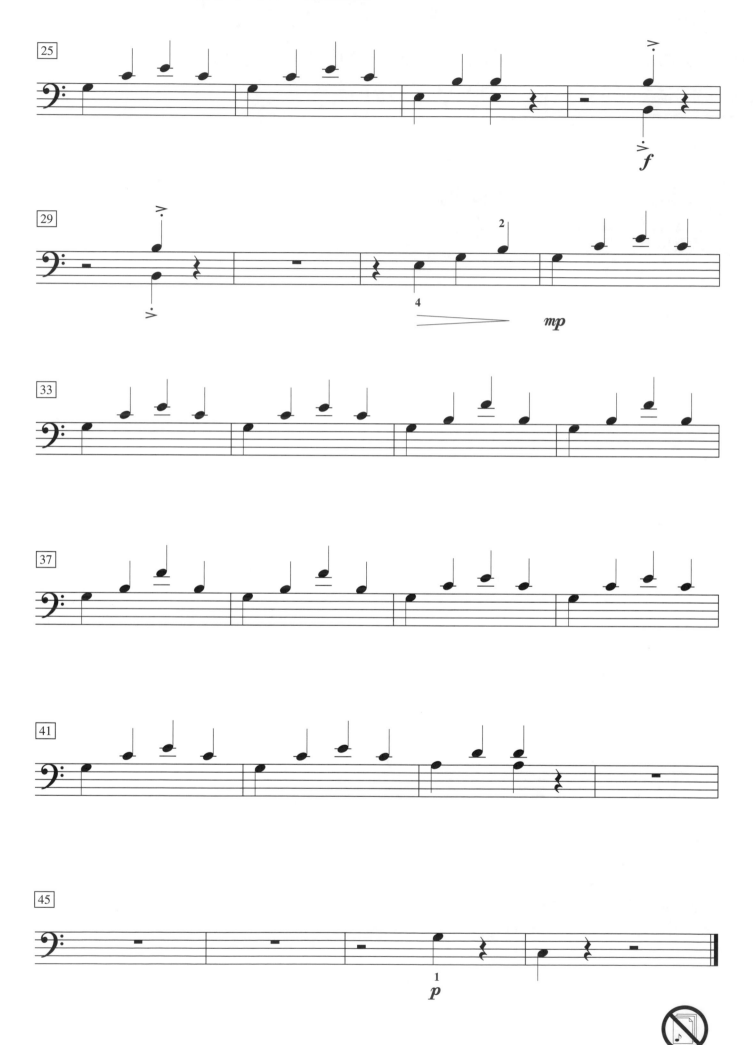

DO NOT PHOTOCOPY

Silver Bells
from the Paramount Picture THE LEMON DROP KID
Part II

If you are:
- sharing the keyboard with *Part I*, **play as written**.
- seated at your own keyboard, **play as written**.

Suggested instrumentation: **bassoon**

Music by Jay Livingston
and Ray Evans
Arranged by Phillip Keveren

Copyright © 1950 (Renewed 1977) by Paramount Music Corporation
This arrangement Copyright © 2004 by Paramount Music Corporation
International Copyright Secured   All Rights Reserved

DO NOT PHOTOCOPY

If you are:
• sharing the keyboard with *Part IV*,
  play as written.
• seated at your own keyboard,
  play as written.

Suggested instrumentation:
clarinet

Parade Of The
Wooden Soldiers

Part III

Music by Leon Jessel
Arranged by Phillip Keveren

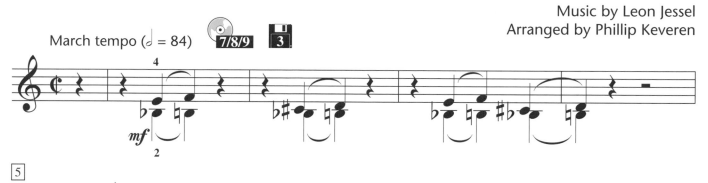

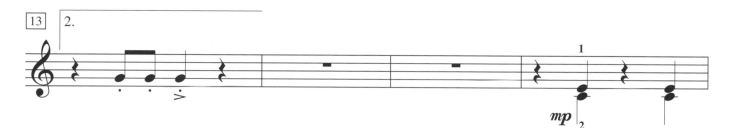

DO NOT PHOTOCOPY

Copyright © 2004 by HAL LEONARD CORPORATION
International Copyright Secured   All Rights Reserved

Christmas Piano Ensembles – Level 4

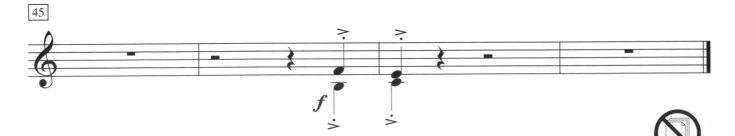

DO NOT PHOTOCOPY

If you are:
- sharing the keyboard with *Part IV*, **play as written**.
- seated at your own keyboard, **play as written**.

Suggested instrumentation:
piano

Silver Bells
from the Paramount Picture THE LEMON DROP KID

Part III

Music by Jay Livingston
and Ray Evans
Arranged by Phillip Keveren

Copyright © 1950 (Renewed 1977) by Paramount Music Corporation
This arrangement Copyright © 2004 by Paramount Music Corporation
International Copyright Secured   All Rights Reserved

DO NOT PHOTOCOPY

If you are:
- sharing the keyboard with *Part III*, **play as written**.
- seated at your own keyboard, **play as written**.

Suggested instrumentation:
tuba

Parade Of The Wooden Soldiers

Part IV

Music by Leon Jessel
Arranged by Phillip Keveren

Copyright © 2004 by HAL LEONARD CORPORATION
International Copyright Secured   All Rights Reserved

DO NOT PHOTOCOPY

DO NOT PHOTOCOPY

Copyright © 1950 (Renewed 1977) by Paramount Music Corporation
This arrangement Copyright © 2004 by Paramount Music Corporation
International Copyright Secured All Rights Reserved

DO NOT PHOTOCOPY

PIANO ENSEMBLES FROM THE
HAL LEONARD STUDENT PIANO LIBRARY

PIANO ENSEMBLES SERIES

arranged by Phillip Keveren

These ensembles feature student favorites correlated from Books 1-5 of the Hal Leonard Student Piano Library. Each book in the Piano Ensembles series contains four selections which include:

- Four individual student parts for each song on perforated tear-out sheets
- Conductor's score with optional teacher accompaniment
- Performance configurations for two or more pianos
- Suggested instrumentation for digital keyboards

Also available are Orchestrated Arrangements on CD or GM Disk

LEVEL 1
Includes: Go for the Gold • Night Shadows • Party Cat • Trumpet Man.
_____ 00296064 Book $5.95
_____ 00296073 CD $5.95
_____ 00296074 GM Disk $9.95

LEVEL 2
Includes: Basketball Bounce • Painted Rocking Horse • Stompin' • Summer Evenings.
_____ 00296065 Book $5.95
_____ 00296075 CD $5.95
_____ 00296076 GM Disk $9.95

LEVEL 3
Includes: Dixieland Jam • Fresh Start • Scherzo • Street Fair.
_____ 00296066 Book $5.95
_____ 00296077 CD $5.95
_____ 00296078 GM Disk $9.95

LEVEL 4
Includes: Allegro from *Eine Kleine Nachtmusik* • Calypso Cat • Carpet Ride • Jig.
_____ 00296067 Book $5.95
_____ 00296079 CD $5.95
_____ 00296080 GM Disk $9.95

LEVEL 5
Includes: Gypsy Song • A Minor Contribution • Wade in the Water • A Whispered Promise.
_____ 00296090 Book $5.95
_____ 00296091 CD $5.95
_____ 00296092 GM Disk $9.95

CHRISTMAS PIANO ENSEMBLES

arranged by Phillip Keveren

Four-part student ensembles, expertly arranged for two or more pianos. These ensembles feature favorite Christmas carols and hymns in graded books that correspond directly to the HLSPL Piano Method levels. Each book in the Christmas Piano Ensemble series contains four selections which include:

- Four individual student parts for each song on perforated tear-out sheets
- Conductor's score with optional teacher accompaniment
- Performance configurations for two or more pianos
- Suggested instrumentation for digital keyboards

Also available are Orchestrated Arrangements on CD or GM Disk

LEVEL 1
Includes: Good King Wenceslas • Jolly Old St. Nicholas • We Three Kings of Orient Are.
_____ 00296338 Book $6.95
_____ 00296343 CD $10.95
_____ 00296348 GM Disk $12.95

LEVEL 2
Includes: I Saw Three Ships • O Come, All Ye Faithful (Adeste Fideles) • What Child Is This?
_____ 00296339 Book $6.95
_____ 00296344 CD $10.95
_____ 00296349 GM Disk $12.95

LEVEL 3
Includes: Carol of the Bells • Rockin' Around the Christmas Tree • Rudolph the Red-Nosed Reindeer • We Wish You a Merry Christmas.
_____ 00296340 Book $6.95
_____ 00296345 CD $10.95
_____ 00296350 GM Disk $12.95

LEVEL 4
Includes: Angels We Have Heard on High • Jingle-Bell Rock • Parade of the Wooden Soldiers • Silver Bells.
_____ 00296341 Book $6.95
_____ 00296346 CD $10.95
_____ 00296351 GM Disk $12.95

LEVEL 5
Includes: Jingle Bells • Let It Snow! Let It Snow! Let It Snow! • March from *The Nutcracker* • Mister Santa.
_____ 00296342 Book $6.95
_____ 00296347 CD $10.95
_____ 00296352 GM Disk $12.95

COMPOSER SHOWCASE ENSEMBLES

WORLD GEMS
Folk Songs for Piano Ensemble
by Amy O'Grady
Level 4 (Early Intermediate)
Fostering collaboration between teacher and students, these six arrangements of familiar international folksongs create exciting sonorities for digital keyboards and/or pianos. Two- and three-part ensembles with student parts and conductor's score. Titles include: African Nöel • Choucounne • El Condor Pasa • Jasmine Flower Song • Mexican Hat Dance (Jarabe Tapatio) • Sakura (Cherry Blossoms).

_____ 00296505 Book $6.95

ROMP!
by Phillip Keveren
Digital Keyboard Ensemble (6 keyboards/6 players)
Sure to inspire students and thrill audiences, this vigorous composition is both blisteringly hot and *way cool* at the same time! Scored for six players at six digital keyboards, the piece was commissioned in 2002 by the Indiana Music Teachers Association and the Music Teachers National Association.

_____ 00296549 Book/CD $7.95
_____ 00296548 Book/GM Disk $9.95

FOR MORE INFORMATION, SEE YOUR LOCAL MUSIC DEALER,
OR WRITE TO:

HAL•LEONARD®
CORPORATION

7777 W. BLUEMOUND RD. P.O. BOX 13819 MILWAUKEE, WI 53213

www.halleonard.com

Prices, contents, and availability subject to change without notice.
Prices may vary outside the U.S.A.